NATIONAL GEOGRAPHIC
School Publishing

T0042416

Where People Live

Scott White

PICTURE CREDITS
Cover, 5 (above), 15 (above), Lonely Planet Images; 1, 2, 4 (above), 5 (below), 7 (right), 8, 9 (below), 10, 11 (all), 13 (right), 14 (above left, above right & below right), Photolibrary.com; 4 (below), 12, 13 (left), 14 (below left), 15 (center left), APL/Corbis; 6, Jeff Greenberg/PhotoEdit, Inc.; 7 (left), 9 (above right), 15 (center right & below), Getty Images.

Produced through the worldwide resources of the National Geographic Society, John M. Fahey, Jr., President and Chief Executive Officer; Gilbert M. Grosvenor, Chairman of the Board; Nina D. Hoffman, Executive Vice President and President, Books and Education Publishing Group.

PREPARED BY NATIONAL GEOGRAPHIC SCHOOL PUBLISHING
Ericka Markman, Senior Vice President and President Children's Books and Education Publishing Group; Steve Mico, Senior Vice President and Publisher; Marianne Hiland, Editorial Director; Lynnette Brent, Executive Editor; Michael Murphy and Barbara Wood, Senior Editors; Bea Jackson, Design Director; David Dumo, Art Director; Margaret Sidlowsky, Illustrations Director; Matt Wascavage, Manager of Publishing Services; Sean Philpotts, Production Manager.

MANUFACTURING AND QUALITY MANAGEMENT
Christopher A. Liedel, Chief Financial Officer; Phillip L. Schlosser, Director; Clifton M. Brown III, Manager.

BOOK DEVELOPMENT
Ibis for Kids Australia Pty Limited.

Copyright © 2006 National Geographic Society. All rights reserved. Reproduction of the whole or any part of the contents without written permission from the publisher is prohibited. National Geographic, National Geographic *Windows on Literacy*, and the Yellow Border are registered trademarks of the National Geographic Society.

Published by the National Geographic Society
1145 17th Street, N.W.
Washington, D.C. 20036-4688

ISBN: 0-7922-6070-8

Third Printing 2007
Printed in China

Contents

Think and Discuss	4
Living in Hot Places	6
Living in Cold Places	8
Living in Wet Places	10
Living in Dry Places	12
Use What You Learned	14
Index	16

Think and Discuss

People live in many different places.
Talk about these different places.

Living in Hot Places

Some people live in hot places.
How do people live in these places?

People need shade in hot places.

This woman's clothes help protect her from the hot sun.

People use fans to keep cool.

Living in Cold Places

Some people live in cold places.
How do people live in these places?

These clothes help the children keep warm.

This house has a fire to help people keep warm.

This snowplow clears a road.

Living in Wet Places

Some people live in wet places.
How do people live in these places?

Some people build houses on stilts.

Sometimes people use umbrellas to stay dry.

Some people use boats as shops.

Living in Dry Places

Some people live in dry places.
How do people live in these places?

People use this water tank to catch water when it rains.

People get water from this well in the ground.

This pipe brings water from far away.

Use What You Learned

Talk about these pictures.
What do they show you about different places?

cold

cool

dry

hot

house

live

place

water

wet

Index

boat 11

fan 7

fire 9

shade 6

snowplow 9

stilts 10

umbrella 11

water tank 12

well 12